DISCUSSING THE
DA VINCI
CODE

Other Resources by Lee Strobel and Garry Poole

Experiencing the Passion of Jesus

Exploring the Da Vinci Code

Faith Under Fire 1, Faith and Jesus (participant's guide, DVD, and leader's guide)

Faith Under Fire 2, Faith and Facts (participant's guide, DVD, and leader's guide)

Faith Under Fire 3, Tough Faith Questions (participant's guide, DVD, and leader's guide)

Faith Under Fire 4, A New Kind of Faith (participant's guide, DVD, and leader's guide)

Other Resources by Lee Strobel

The Case for Christ

The Case for Christ audio

The Case for Christ—Student Edition (with Jane Vogel)

The Case for Christmas

The Case for a Creator

The Case for a Creator audio

The Case for Creator—Student Edition (with Jane Vogel)

The Case for Easter

The Case for Faith

The Case for Faith audio

The Case for Faith—Student Edition (with Jane Vogel)

God's Outrageous Claims

Inside the Mind of Unchurched Harry and Mary

Surviving a Spiritual Mismatch in Marriage (with Leslie Strobel)

Surviving a Spiritual Mismatch in Marriage audio

What Jesus Would Say

Other Resources by Garry Poole

The Complete Book of Questions

Seeker Small Groups

The Three Habits of Highly Contagious Christians

In the Tough Questions Series:

Don't All Religions Lead to God?

How Could God Allow Suffering and Evil?

How Does Anyone Know God Exists?

Why Become a Christian?

Tough Questions Leader's Guide (with Judson Poling)

EXAMINING THE ISSUES RAISED BY THE BOOK & MOVIE

DISCUSSING THE
DA VINCI
CODE

LEE
STROBEL

GARRY
POOLE

ZONDERVAN™

GRAND RAPIDS, MICHIGAN 49530 USA

ZONDERVAN.COM/
AUTHORTRACKER

We want to hear from you. Please send your comments about this book to us in care of zreview@zondervan.com. Thank you.

ZONDERVAN™

Discussing the Da Vinci Code
Copyright © 2006 by Lee Strobel and Garry Poole

Requests for information should be addressed to:
Zondervan, *Grand Rapids, Michigan 49530*

ISBN-10: 0-310-27265-3
ISBN-13: 978-0-310-27265-6

All Scripture quotations, unless otherwise indicated, are taken from the *Holy Bible: New International Version®*. NIV®. Copyright © 1973, 1978, 1984 by International Bible Society. Used by permission of Zondervan. All rights reserved.

All quotations from *The Da Vinci Code* are from the Doubleday hardcover edition, © 2003 by Dan Brown.

The website addresses recommended throughout this book are offered as a resource to you. These websites are not intended in any way to be or imply an endorsement on the part of Zondervan, nor do we vouch for their content for the life of this book.

Interior design by Beth Shagene

Printed in the United States of America

06 07 08 09 10 11 12 • 19 18 17 16 15 14 13 12 11 10 9 8 7 6 5 4 3 2

CONTENTS

PREFACE

On an airplane over Iowa:

> PASSENGER #1: You're a Christian too? So am I. That's great.
> PASSENGER #2: Yeah, that's great.
>   (pause)
> PASSENGER #1: I just read *The Da Vinci Code.* Have you read it?
> PASSENGER #2: Sure did.
> PASSENGER #1: What percentage do you think is true?
>   (pause)
> PASSENGER #2: Oh, about 80 percent.

Dan Brown's red-hot page-turner *The Da Vinci Code* has become a runaway bestseller. What's most intriguing to me, though, is not merely the astronomical sales figures, but the effect the book is having on popular culture. By cleverly mixing fact with fiction, Brown has created a raging controversy over how many of the novel's claims are rooted in reality. One study showed that one out of three Canadians who have read the book now believes descendants of Jesus are walking among us today!

If true, the book's assertions are nothing less than breathtaking: Jesus was merely a human being, Christianity is a fraud, and the four Gospels in the Bible are unreliable. But are those stunning allegations actually supported by historical evidence? Or are they as fanciful as the colorful characters in Brown's novel?

I'm glad you're interested in getting to the bottom of these important issues. *Discussing the Da Vinci Code* is designed to help you investigate the major themes of Brown's book and movie in the safe context of a spirited conversation. You'll be encouraged to offer your opinions and thoughts, and you'll have the opportunity to weigh the perspectives of other group members. In the end, I hope you'll come to your own well-reasoned conclusions about the claims of *The Da Vinci Code*.

When I was an atheist and began my own probe into the case for Christianity, I promised myself that I would maintain an open mind—and I hope you'll make that same resolution as you begin your journey into exploring this controversial book and film. I believe you'll find the topics in this discussion guide to be fascinating:

- What can history really tell us?
- Can we trust the four Gospels?
- What's the role of women in Christianity?
- Is Jesus the Son of God?

You'll hear from leading experts, all of them with doctorates in relevant areas, as I interview them about not only what they believe but why they believe it. You'll even see footage of some of the key sites where the novel unfolds in France and England. And at the end of each session, I'll offer my own thoughts for you to consider.

The truth is, there is a lot at stake: can Jesus really be trusted as God incarnate, or was he merely a human pawn in the greatest scam in history? So engage, analyze, converse, ponder, study, grapple, contemplate, debate, learn, deliberate, grow—and then decide for yourself.

Have a great time discussing *The Da Vinci Code*! And be sure to visit the Web site: *www.discussingthedavincicode.com*.

Lee Strobel

8

GETTING STARTED

You will seek me and find me when you seek me with all your heart.
Jeremiah 29:13

Christianity maintains that God welcomes sincere examination and inquiry; in fact, it's a matter of historical record that Jesus encouraged such scrutiny. The Bible is not a secret kept only for the initiated few, but an open book, available for study and debate. The teachings of Christ are freely offered to all—the skeptic as well as the believer.

So here's an open invitation: examine the claims, explore the options, and draw your own conclusions. In an atmosphere of honest seeking and unrestricted discussion, we challenge you to put the claims of Christianity—as well as your own beliefs—to the test. We trust you'll find *Discussing the Da Vinci Code* to be a useful guide in facilitating this journey of spiritual discovery.

Of course, it's possible for any of us to believe error; it is also feasible for us to resist truth. My hope is that this discussion guide will help you and your friends sort out truth from speculation, and facts from opinion. I'm convinced it is healthy for all of us to wrestle with the assertions of the New Testament so we can make an informed decision about the relevance of Jesus to our personal lives.

A Safe Place
for Tough Questions

Discussing the Da Vinci Code is designed to give both spiritual seekers and Christians a chance to raise questions and investigate themes related to the most provocative claims of *The Da Vinci Code*, both the book and the movie. If you've read Dan Brown's powerful and captivating book or seen the film, then undoubtedly significant issues have arisen in your mind concerning the authenticity of historical Christianity, the reliability of the Gospels, the role of women in the church, and the true identity of Jesus. Your comments, questions, and concerns—even your objections—will be fully welcomed in the safe context of a small group discussion based on this guide.

Since the primary audience for this guide is the not-yet-convinced seekers, the ideal place to use *Discussing the Da Vinci Code* is within the context of seeker small groups. These groups consist of several people who are interested in investigating faith issues, along with a Christian or two who have volunteered to lead the discussions. These groups gather on a regular basis, perhaps weekly, at homes, offices, restaurants, churches—even Starbucks! The greatest hope behind the publication of this guide is that spiritual seekers everywhere will be encouraged in a respectful way to seriously consider the claims of Christ—and then to reach their own independent and well-informed decisions about how to respond.

This guide is also designed for small groups of Christians to use as they discuss answers to the tough questions that skeptics and seekers are asking about Brown's book. The process of tackling these important issues will not only fortify their own faith, but will also provide them with insights for entering into dialogues about Christianity with their seeking friends, colleagues, neighbors, and family members.

Features of the Curriculum

Discussing the Da Vinci Code includes four distinct sessions, each with several short DVD clips; about fifteen questions to draw out group interaction; and numerous quotes to stimulate thinking. Your group may find it challenging to get through all the material within each discussion in just one sitting. That's okay. The important thing is to engage in the topic at hand—not to necessarily get through every question—although it's ideal to cover enough of each session's content that everyone has some sense of closure. Your group may even decide to spend more than one meeting on each session in order to complete all the information addressed.

The discussion questions are intended to elicit spirited dialogue rather than short, simple answers. Strictly speaking, this guide is not a Bible study, though it regularly refers to biblical themes and passages. Instead, it is a topical discussion guide, meant to get you talking about what you really think and feel. The sessions have a point and attempt to lead to some resolution, but they fall short of providing the last word on any of the questions raised. That is left for you to discover for yourself! You will be invited to bring your experiences, perspectives, and uncertainties to the discussion, and you will also be challenged to compare your beliefs with what the Bible teaches in order to determine where you stand as each meeting unfolds.

Leading the Discussions

Each group should have a leader—not to lecture, but to create an engaging experience in which all viewpoints are welcomed. The book, *Seeker Small Groups*, is strongly recommended as a useful resource for leaders to learn how to effectively start up small groups and facilitate discussions for spiritual seekers. *The Complete Book of Questions: 1001 Conversation Starters for Any Occasion*, a resource filled with icebreaker questions, may be a helpful tool to assist everyone in your group to get to know one another better and more easily launch your group interactions.

Keep the following list of suggestions in mind as you prepare to lead the discussions:

- If possible, read over the material to be discussed before each meeting. Familiarity with the topic will greatly enrich the time you spend in the discussion.
- Use a modern translation of the Bible, such as the New International Version. You might prefer to use a Bible that includes notes especially for seekers, such as *The Journey: A Bible for the Spiritually Curious*.
- Be sure to make the necessary arrangements to view the *Discussing the Da Vinci Code* DVD clips during your gathering, as indicated. These clips are specifically designed to enhance the quality of your group interactions.

For further help in leading a discussion session for this book, see Appendix 4: For Leaders Only on pages 93–94.

Participating in the Discussions

Like the leader, you'll get the most out of each session when you're prepared. Keep the following list of suggestions in mind as you prepare to participate in the discussions:

- Be willing to join in the group discussion. The leader of the group will not present a sermon, but will invite each of you to openly discuss your opinions and disagreements. Plan to share your ideas honestly and forthrightly.
- Be sensitive to the other members of your group. Listen attentively when they speak and be affirming whenever you can. This will motivate more hesitant members to

participate. Always show respect toward the others, even if they don't agree with your position.

- Be careful not to dominate the discussion. By all means participate, but allow others to have equal time.
- Try to stick to the topic being studied. There won't be enough time to handle the peripheral matters that come to mind during the meeting. However, these might provide fodder for further discussions outside the regular meeting.
- Do some extra reading in the Bible and other recommended books as you work through these sessions. To get you started, we've included Appendix 1: Recommended Resources on page 81.
- One last suggestion: at the outset, even if you're not sure God exists, whisper a prayer. If you have doubts, tell him. If you're skeptical, let him know. But then ask him to reveal himself to you—and express your willingness to respond to him if and when he does.

The Challenge

Christianity stands or falls on Christ. And yet he left us with a lot of hard sayings. But the central scandal of Christianity is that at a point in history, God came down to live among us in a person, Jesus of Nazareth. And the most baffling moment of Jesus' life was on the cross—where he hung to die like a common criminal. In that place of weakness—where all seemed lost, where the taunts of "Prove yourself, Jesus, and come down from there!" lashed out like the whip that flogged him prior to his crucifixion—somehow God was at his best. There at the cross, he expressed a love greater than words could ever describe. That act of Jesus, presented as the ultimate demonstration of the love and justice of God, begs to be put to "cross" examination.

As you grapple with the important spiritual issues raised in this guide I'm convinced that you'll find satisfying, reasonable answers to your most challenging questions. And you're invited to discover them with others in your small group discussions. Engage fully and sincerely with your whole heart and mind—and get ready for an adventure of the mind and spirit!

Garry Poole

Seek and you will find;
knock and the door will be opened to you.
Matthew 7:7

WHAT CAN HISTORY REALLY TELL US?

Blinding ignorance does mislead us.
O! Wretched mortals, open your eyes!
Leonardo da Vinci

Watch It! (DVD Clip #1, 1 minute)

In this brief video segment, Lee Strobel introduces the discussion topic for this session. Use the following space to take a few notes.

Discuss It!

1 What was your overall reaction to *The Da Vinci Code*? What did you like most about the book? Least? Give reasons for your answers.

2 What questions, issues, or concerns about historical Christianity does *The Da Vinci Code* raise in your mind?

3 Can historical events be verified? Why or why not? What do you think determines whether or not an historical event actually occurred?

Watch It! (DVD Clip #2, 7 minutes)

Use the following space to take notes as Lee Strobel interviews historian Paul Maier about: history being written by "winners," the reliability of historical documents, and the Priory of Sion. Dr. Maier, a professor of ancient history at Western Michigan University, has written over 250 scholarly articles and reviews in professional journals. His books include *In the Fullness of Time*, which examines secular evidence for Jesus; a new translation and commentary of the first-century historian Josephus; and a study of Eusebius, the first Christian historian. He also has written three novels, including *A Skeleton in God's Closet*, a number-one national bestseller in religious fiction.

Discuss It!

4 *The Da Vinci Code* says that "history is always written by the winners. When two cultures clash, the loser is obliterated, and the winner writes the history books—books which glorify their own cause and disparage the conquered foe" (p. 256). Do you agree or disagree? Why?

Gauging Historical Accuracy

"Many historians now believe (as do I) that in gauging the historical accuracy of a given concept, we should first ask ourselves a far deeper question: How historically accurate is history itself?"

Dan Brown

5 In their book *Cracking Da Vinci's Code*, James Garlow and Peter Jones ask, "If everything Brown presents in *The Da Vinci Code* is 'historical fact,' who are the new 'winners' he relies on for his historical facts?" How would you answer their question? Explain your response.

Objective Truth?

"We always see and relate events through the prism of perspective. Everyone involved in a car accident has a slightly different version of the events, for example. But that doesn't mean the accident itself *didn't happen*. Despite the limitations of the observers, there is, indeed, an objective truth as to who caused the accident, no matter how difficult it may be to unearth. However, in *The Da Vinci Code*, Brown uses 'history is written by the winners' to suggest that the whole history of Christianity, beginning with Jesus himself, is a lie, written by those who were determined to suppress Jesus' 'real' message. It's not about different interpretations of Jesus' life and message. It's about the basic data itself: that what we read in the New Testament and what records of early Christianity itself exist, aren't accurate presentations of what really happened."

Amy Welborn in *De-Coding Da Vinci*

Da Vinci Blurbs

"A fact-based thriller."
popmatters.com

"A compelling blend of history and page-turning suspense."
Library Journal

"John Grisham teaches you about torts. Tom Clancy teaches you about military technology. Dan Brown gives you a crash course in art history and the Catholic Church."
**Stephen Rubin, president and publisher,
Doubleday/Broadway Publishing Group**

Fact or Fiction?

"Fiction—such as the notion that Christianity was concocted to subjugate women—is being cleverly peddled as fact, while fact—such as the deity of Christ—is being capriciously passed off as fiction."
**Hank Hanegraaff, the "Bible Answer Man,"
in *The Da Vinci Code: Fact or Fiction?***

6 Generally speaking, what percentage of Dan Brown's book do you think is fact and what percentage of it is fiction?

Dan Brown: A Believer

"I began as a skeptic. As I started researching *Da Vinci Code*, I really thought I would disprove a lot of this theory about Mary Magdalene and holy blood and all of that. I became a believer."

Dan Brown to Elizabeth Vargas on ABC's *Primetime Live*

Factual and Accurate?

"One of the many qualities that make *The Da Vinci Code* unique is the factual nature of the story. All the history, artwork, ancient documents, and secret rituals in the novel are accurate, as are the hidden codes revealed in some of da Vinci's most famous paintings."

Dan Brown to Ruth Mariampolski for Borders, Inc.

Grounded in Reality?

Matt Lauer: How much of this book [*The Da Vinci Code*] is based on reality in terms of things that actually occurred?

Dan Brown: Absolutely all of it. Obviously Robert Langdon is fictional, but all of the art, architecture, secret rituals, secret societies—all of that is historical fact.

The *Today Show*, NBC, June 9, 2003

Error-Laden?

"So error-laden is *The Da Vinci Code* that the educated reader actually applauds those rare occasions where Brown stumbles (despite himself) into the truth."

Sandra Miesel, *Crisis* magazine

7 Dan Brown begins *The Da Vinci Code* on page 1 by listing the following statements under the heading "FACT":

a. The Priory of Sion—a European secret society founded in 1099—is a real organization.

b. In 1975 Paris's Bibliothèque Nationale discovered parchments known as *Les Dossiers Secrets*, identifying numerous members of the Priory of Sion, including Sir Isaac Newton, Botticelli, Victor Hugo, and Leonardo da Vinci.

c. The Vatican prelature known as Opus Dei is a deeply devout Catholic sect.

According to historians, only one of the preceding statements is historically accurate. Can you identify which one?

Here are the answers:

a. False. The Priory of Sion was founded in France in 1956.

b. False. The documents do exist, but they were forged and planted there by Pierre Plantard, who later admitted the documents were phony.

c. True.

If two of the three statements from Brown's FACT page are actually false, what does this tell you about the accuracy of the rest of the book's claims? Explain.

The Priory of Sion

"The Priory of Sion, according to *The Da Vinci Code*, is one of the oldest secret societies still in existence. It is the Priory that has been charged with guarding the secret of the true Holy Grail, starting in 1099 when the Knights Templar discovered long-lost documents beneath the ruins of Solomon's Temple. Leonardo da Vinci was Grand Master of this society, says Robert Langdon, from 1510 to 1519. The only problem is this: It is all a hoax.

"Brown relies on a 1982 publication, *Holy Blood, Holy Grail*, for his information on the Priory of Sion. The authors of *Holy Blood, Holy Grail* relied on documents provided them by Pierre Plantard, who spent time in jail for fraud in 1953. Plantard and three other men started a small social club in 1956 called the Priory of Sion, taking the name from a nearby mountain. Their club's 'cause' was the call for more low-cost housing in France. The club dissolved in 1957, but Plantard held on to the name.

"Throughout the 1960s and the 1970s, Plantard created a series of documents 'proving' the existence of a bloodline descending from Mary Magdalene, through the kings of France, down to the present day to include (surprise!) Pierre Plantard. He began using the name Plantard de Saint-Clair, saying the Saint-Clairs were direct descendants of the line of Jesus and Mary.

"In 1993, Plantard's name came up in light of a political scandal involving a close friend of then French president François Mitterand. When called upon to testify, Plantard, under oath, admitted he had made up the whole Priory scheme."

James Garlow and Peter Jones in *Cracking Da Vinci's Code*

8 Read the following examples of other inaccuracies found in *The Da Vinci Code*. What impact do these relatively minor distortions have on your level of confidence in other more substantial claims made throughout the book?

- According to *The Da Vinci Code* (p. 21), the pyramid outside the Louvre in Paris has 666 panes of glass. But according to the official Web site of the Louvre Museum, the pyramid is covered in 673 diamond-shaped panes.
- According to *The Da Vinci Code* (pp. 36–37), the Greeks based their Olympic games on an eight-year cycle as a tribute to the planet Venus, which represented a goddess. In reality, the Olympics were held in honor of the Greek god Zeus on a four-year cycle.
- According to *The Da Vinci Code* (p. 257), the Merovingian royal family founded Paris. But Paris was established by a tribe of Celtic Gauls called the Parisii in the third century BC. The Merovingians made Paris the capital of the Frankish kingdom in AD 508.

Trustworthy?

"The Da Vinci Code clearly contains many historical errors covering a wide variety of issues: church architecture, religious symbolism, the Roman Empire, ancient Israel, and different spiritual belief systems. If Brown cannot be relied upon to accurately recount the most basic of historical facts, then how can he be trusted to correctly explain more complex subjects?"

Richard Abanes in *The Truth Behind the Da Vinci Code*

9 Listed below are some of *The Da Vinci Code*'s many controversial claims disputed by numerous biblical scholars and historians. To what extent do you think people view these controversial theories as factual? Generally speaking, how do you view these theories? Check any that you consider to be accurate. Why?

- ☐ The Bible was put together by Constantine, a pagan Roman emperor. (p. 231)
- ☐ The Gospels have been edited to support the claims of later Christians. (p. 234)
- ☐ Jesus is not the Son of God; he was only a man. (pp. 233–235)
- ☐ Jesus was not viewed as God until the fourth century, when he was deified by the Emperor Constantine. (pp. 233–234)
- ☐ Jesus was married to Mary Magdalene. (pp. 242–250)
- ☐ In the original Gospels, Mary Magdalene, not Peter, was directed to establish the church. (p. 254)
- ☐ Mary Magdalene was to be worshiped as a goddess. (p. 255)
- ☐ There is a secret society known as the Priory of Sion that still worships Mary Magdalene as a goddess and is trying to keep that practice alive. (p. 255)
- ☐ Jesus and Mary Magdalene conceived a child and named her Sarah. (p. 255)
- ☐ Sarah gave rise to a prominent family line that is still present in Europe today. (pp. 257–258)
- ☐ The Catholic Church often has assassinated the descendants of Christ to keep his bloodline from growing. (p. 266)

The Da Vinci Code Excerpts

- "It would not be the first time in history the Church has killed to protect itself. The documents that accompany the Holy Grail are explosive, and the Church has wanted to destroy them for years." (p. 266)
- "Mary Magdalene was pregnant at the time of the crucifixion.... She had no choice but to flee the Holy Land.... She gave birth to a daughter. Her name was Sarah." (p. 255)
- "The Church has two thousand years of experience pressuring those who threaten to unveil its lies.... The Church may no longer employ crusaders to slaughter non-believers, but their influence is ... no less insidious." (p. 407)
- "Almost everything our fathers taught us about Christ is *false*." (p. 235)

10 Do you think that Christianity, as we know it, is a fabrication, and that the truth has been repressed?

History Mixed with Falsehoods

"This is a good airplane book, a novelistic thriller that presents a rummage sale of accurate historical nuggets alongside falsehoods and misleading statements. The bottom line: The book should come coded for 'black light,' like the pen used by the character Saunière to record his dying words so that readers could scan pages to see which 'facts' are trustworthy and which patently not."

Margaret M. Mitchell, chair of the Department of New Testament and Early Christian Literature at the University of Chicago

Watch It! (DVD Clip #3, 7 minutes)

Use the following space to take notes as Lee Strobel continues to interview history expert Paul Maier on: the historical claims about Constantine, why people take *The Da Vinci Code* as factual, and Dan Brown's agenda.

Discuss It!

11 If there are so many fallacies contained within *The Da Vinci Code*, why do you think so many people accept the book as a story based on facts and actual historical events?

12 The following phrases are peppered throughout Brown's book:

Religious historians	Well-documented history
Art historians	All academics
Real historians	Well-documented evidence
Scores of historians	Historical evidence

In what ways do such phrases give credibility and legitimacy to Dan Brown's story? If the book's assertions are not really based on actual research, are such statements misleading? Why or why not?

Fiction Indeed?

"Be it said to Brown's credit: the literary category for *Da Vinci* is fiction indeed."

Paul Maier in *The Da Vinci Code: Fact or Fiction?*

13 Do you think Dan Brown had an agenda in writing *The Da Vinci Code*? Why or why not? If so, what do you think it was?

Lessons from Dan Brown

"Two thousand years ago, we lived in a world of Gods and Goddesses. Today we live in a world solely of Gods. Women in most cultures have been stripped of their spiritual power. The novel touches on questions of how and why this shift occurred ... and on what lessons we might learn from it regarding our future."

Dan Brown at *danbrown.com*

14 Amy Welborn suggests that authors of historical fiction make an implicit deal with the reader that, while the novel concerns fictional characters engaged in imagined activities, the basic historical framework is correct. But in *The Da Vinci Code*, imaginative detail and false historical assertions are presented as facts and the fruit of serious historical research. Do you agree with Welborn that such an "implicit deal" exists between authors of historical fiction and their readers? Why or why not? In reading a work of historical fiction, how important is it that the novel portray history accurately?

It Didn't Happen?

"Brown claims that Jesus wanted the movement that followed him to be about a greater awareness of the 'sacred feminine.' He says that this movement, under the leadership and inspiration of Mary Magdalene, thrived during the first three centuries until it was brutally suppressed by the Emperor Constantine. *There's no evidence to suggest that this is true. It didn't happen....* Credible scholarly sources also suggest that much of Brown's other assertions—about everything from the nature of the Grail myth to the Priory of Sion to the role of goddess worship in the ancient world—just aren't supported by the evidence that's out there."

Amy Welborn in *De-Coding Da Vinci*

15 Some people assert that *The Da Vinci Code* is just a novel with no harm done. Others have a problem with the way Dan Brown, his publisher, and the media present *The Da Vinci Code* as a fact-based exposé that purports to teach history and reveal truths within the framework of fiction. In your opinion, is *The Da Vinci Code* just a novel with no harm done or is it cause for alarm? Why or why not?

16 In the *National Review*, David Klinghoffer wrote, "What's at stake in *The Da Vinci Code* is nothing less than traditional Christianity itself." Do you think that *The Da Vinci Code* poses any real threat to Christianity? Why or why not?

Watch It! (DVD Clip #4, 2 minutes)

Lee's Perspective

Every trial I covered as a legal journalist investigated an event of recent history. Did the defendant murder the victim? Did the doctor commit malpractice? To determine the truth, jurors consider eyewitness testimony, study documents, examine physical evidence—and through it all, they rely on their own common sense. In a way, the study of ancient evidence is the same. Do we have records that are rooted in eyewitness accounts and are close to the events themselves? Does archaeology corroborate or contradict the testimony? By carefully examining the evidence and using our common sense, we can conclude with reasonable certainty whether an event occurred long ago.

When I apply those standards to the historical claims of *The Da Vinci Code*, I walk away totally unconvinced that they're rooted in reality. They simply do not hold up to sober scrutiny. However, when I devoted two years of my life, as an atheist, to investigating the life and resurrection of Jesus, I became absolutely convinced that Jesus is the unique Son of God who proved it by returning from the dead. So let me ask this: where do *you* believe that the historical evidence points—and why?

CAN WE TRUST THE FOUR GOSPELS?

Many have made a trade of delusions
and false miracles, deceiving the stupid multitude.
Leonardo da Vinci

Watch It! (DVD Clip #1, 1 minute)

In this brief video segment, Lee Strobel introduces the discussion topic for this session. Use the following space to take a few notes.

Discuss It!

1 Growing up, what do you remember hearing or believing about the Bible? Did you readily believe what you were told, or did you tend to be skeptical about its contents?

Faith and Metaphors

"Every religion describes God through metaphor, allegory, and exaggeration, from the early Egyptians through modern Sunday school.... The problems arise when we begin to believe literally in our own metaphors." (pp. 341–342)
The Da Vinci Code

2 Select the statement(s) that best describe your current view of the Bible. Give reasons to support your view.

- ☐ The Bible has no relevance for me.
- ☐ The Bible is an interesting religious book, but it is a mixture of human truth and human error.
- ☐ The Bible is no different from other writings that claim to come from God.
- ☐ The Bible has remarkable wisdom, but that doesn't mean it's God's Word.
- ☐ The Bible has a lot of value and God works through it, but that doesn't mean it's the only book God uses.
- ☐ The Bible is inspired by God, but not the only book inspired by him.
- ☐ The Bible contains God's truths, yet not everything in it is from God.
- ☐ The Bible—all of it, and only it—is God's Word through the words of men.

- ☐ Other: _____

Watch It! (DVD Clip #2, 7 minutes)

Use the following space to take notes as Lee Strobel interviews Gospel expert Scot McKnight on: the reliability of the New Testament, the gospels that didn't make it into the Bible, and how the canon was formed. Dr. McKnight is a professor at North Park University in Chicago. He earned his doctorate at the University of Nottingham and is the author of ten books, including *The Jesus Creed* and *Embracing Grace*. He is a nationally recognized expert on Jesus studies.

Discuss It!

3 Read the following quote from Dan Brown's book:

> "The Bible is a product of *man*, my dear. Not of God....
> Man created it as a historical record of tumultuous times, and
> it has evolved through countless translations, additions, and revisions.
> History has never had a definitive version of the book." (p. 231)

How does *The Da Vinci Code* portray the Bible? Do you believe the Bible was written by God, people, or a combination of the two? Explain.

A Hybrid Religion?

"Constantine was a very good businessman. He could see that Christianity was on the rise, and he simply backed the winning horse." (p. 232)

The Da Vinci Code

Some Valid Points

"Three points in *The Da Vinci Code* have some validity. First, there is no doubt that Constantine was a key figure and that his rule was a turning point in Christian history.... Second, the Nicene Creed was an important affirmation in the history of the faith and was, in part, an effort to control what was to be believed.... Third, the collection of texts into an official list that became the canon of Scripture gained momentum in this period. A result of that process was that documents on the other side of this dispute were destroyed, and their influence waned."

Darrell Bock in *Breaking the Da Vinci Code*

The Books of the Bible

"Constantine did not collate the Bible. The Old Testament had been compiled even before Jesus' time. The New Testament's formation began by the end of the first century (about 90 or 100)—almost two hundred years before Constantine. In fact, recognizing which books of the New Testament were authoritative was a century-long process within both the Eastern (based at Constantinople) and Western (based at Rome) churches. They *independently* agreed on which books belonged in the New Testament."

Richard Abanes in *The Truth Behind the Da Vinci Code*

4 *The Da Vinci Code* claims that more than eighty gospels were considered for the New Testament, but only Matthew, Mark, Luke, and John made the cut. It also claims that the New Testament, as we know it today, was collated by the pagan Roman emperor, Constantine the Great. But, according to New Testament scholar Scot McKnight's DVD comments, who determined which Gospels were included in the Bible, and what was the process behind how the Bible was put together? Was he convincing to you? Why or why not?

The Gnostic Gospels

"Some of [Dan Brown's] most important texts are the various Gnostic gospels, which he uncritically accepts as accurate accounts of Jesus' life.... They were late arrivals, which is one reason why church leaders rejected them.... They lacked authority since their authors were neither (a) apostles of Jesus nor (b) persons associated with apostles of Jesus.... No one really knows who wrote the texts."

Richard Abanes in *The Truth Behind the Da Vinci Code*

5 Why was it important to establish a canon of Scripture? What was the process of establishing the canon of Scripture and what were the criteria used for which books to include?

The Process

Consider the following brief sketch of how the New Testament canon came to be:

1. Letters from apostles were written and received in the churches; copies were made and circulated.
2. A growing group of books developed that were recognized as inspired Scripture. Important questions for their acceptance included: Was the book written by either an apostle or someone who knew the apostles and thus had the stamp of apostolic authority? Was it in harmony with other accepted doctrine?
3. By the end of the first century, all 27 books in our present canon had been written and received by the churches. Though some of the canonical lists were incomplete, this is not always to be interpreted as the rejection of some books. Often it simply means that some books were unknown in certain areas.
4. A generation after the end of the apostolic age, every book of the New Testament had been cited as authoritative by some church father.
5. Remaining doubts or debates over certain books continued into the fourth century. The first time the list of our 27 books appears is in an Easter letter written by Athanasius in AD 367.
6. The 27 books of our New Testament were ratified by the Council of Hippo (AD 393) and the Third Council of Carthage (AD 397).

Erwin Lutzer in *The Da Vinci Deception*

The Dead Sea Scrolls

"Some of the gospels that Constantine attempted to eradicate managed to survive. The Dead Sea Scrolls were found in the 1950s.... The Vatican, in keeping with their tradition of misinformation, tried very hard to suppress the release of these scrolls." (p. 234)

The Da Vinci Code

"Constantine was not in the business of eradicating any gospels. The Dead Sea Scrolls were discovered in 1947, not the 1950s. And they did not contain any gospels or any references to Jesus."

Historian Paul Maier

"Were it not for the enormous impact of *The Da Vinci Code*, I might be tempted to laugh and shrug off such historical mistakes. As any scholar who has studied the Dead Sea Scrolls will tell you, there isn't anything Christian about them. They are the documents and library of early Jews who lived at the Dead Sea. No Christian documents have been found there. The Dead Sea Scrolls don't 'speak of Christ's ministry' at all."

New Testament scholar Ben Witherington III in *The Gospel Code*

6 What criteria should be used today to evaluate whether or not something warrants inclusion in the Bible?

The Evidence for Reliability

Hank Hanegraaff makes a strong case for the reliability of the Bible, using three areas of evidence:

- **Manuscript Evidence**. The New Testament documents have stronger manuscript support than any other work of classical literature, including works of Homer, Plato, Aristotle, Caesar, and Ticitus. Furthermore, the reliability of the Gospel accounts is confirmed through the eyewitness credentials of the authors. Finally, secular historians—including Josephus (before AD 100), the Roman Tacitus (c. AD 120), the Roman Suetonius (c. AD 110), and the Roman governor Pliny the Younger (c. AD 110)— confirm many of the events, people, places, and customs chronicled in the New Testament.
- **Archaeological Evidence**. Archaeology is a powerful witness to the accuracy of biblical documents, confirming scores of references.
- **Evidence from Messianic Prophecies**. The Bible records predictions of events that could not have been known or predicted by chance or common sense.

Corroborating Evidence?

"Often the same people, places, and events referenced inside Scripture are cited also in nonbiblical materials. These range from a myriad of geographical place names to the hard evidence by archaeology to a host of documents that have come down to us from the ancient world that correlate completely with the biblical evidence."

Paul Maier

7 Generally speaking, what percentage of the Bible do you think is fact and what percentage of it is fiction?

Reconstructed?

"The only textual variants which affect more than a sentence or two (and most affect only individual words or phrases) are John 7:53–8:11 and Mark 16:9–20.... But overall, 97 to 99 percent of the New Testament can be reconstructed beyond any reasonable doubt."

New Testament scholar Craig Blomberg,
author of *The Historical Reliability of the Gospels*

8 To what extent do you consider the Bible to be reliable and God's authoritative Word? To what extent do you consider *The Da Vinci Code* to be reliable? In each case, what is the basis for your level of trust or distrust?

Double Standard?

"If the New Testament were a collection of secular writings, their authenticity would generally be regarded as beyond all doubt."

Historian F. F. Bruce, author of
The New Testament Documents: Are They Reliable?

Watch It! (DVD Clip #3, 7 minutes)

Use the following space to take notes as Lee Strobel continues to interview Gospels expert Scot McKnight on: the four Gospels versus the Gnostic gospels, the validation of truth from God, and settling doubts and confusion concerning the Bible.

Discuss It!

9 How do we know the four Gospels are reliable accounts of the life and teachings of Jesus?

10 Some people argue that because the Gospels in the Bible can be traced back to followers of Jesus, the books are biased and contain distorted historical information that agrees with the followers' preconceived notions. Do you agree with this reasoning? Why or why not?

11 It's one thing to say God is speaking through someone, and another thing to substantiate it. What kind of validation would need to be provided by someone who claims to have ultimate truth from God?

12 If God is really behind the Bible, why do you think he hasn't eliminated any doubts or confusion about that?

13 Many people testify to the life-changing message they encounter in the Bible. What are the strengths and weaknesses of using that as a basis for validating the trustworthiness of the Bible? Address the same question regarding *The Da Vinci Code*.

Bible Challenges

"A thousand times over, the death knell of the Bible has been sounded, the funeral procession formed, the inscription cut on the tombstone, and the committal read. But somehow the corpse never stays put."
Bernard Ramm

14 What would motivate you to embark on an investigation to determine once and for all the truth behind *The Da Vinci Code* and the Bible? Where would you begin?

15 What would it take for you to place complete confidence in the Bible as truth from God and as the supreme written guide for your life? What difference would it make in your everyday life to believe that the Bible is God's Word?

Watch It! (DVD Clip #4, 2 minutes)

Lee's Perspective

The four Gospels of the New Testament even managed to convince an atheist like me that they are accurate records of the life, miracles, teachings, death, and resurrection of Jesus. First, I concluded that there's solid evidence that they are rooted in eyewitness testimony. Second, they were written so close to the events that they couldn't be the product of legendary development. Third, they contain embarrassing material about the disciples and hard-to-explain sayings by Jesus that would have been edited out if the writers felt the freedom to manipulate or whitewash the record. Fourth, archaeology and ancient writings outside the Bible tend to corroborate their accuracy. None of the later and fanciful apocryphal gospels come anywhere close to matching their credentials. Even the critical German scholar Peter Stuhlmacher said recently: "We have good reasons to treat the Gospels seriously as a source of information on the life and teachings of Jesus, and thus on the historical origins of Christianity."

I'd encourage anyone, including you, to investigate the credentials of the four Gospels with an open mind—and then ask yourself this life-changing question: "What is the central message that these ancient writings have for me personally?"

WHAT'S THE ROLE OF WOMEN IN CHRISTIANITY?

You do ill if you praise, but worse if you censure,
what you do not understand.
Leonardo da Vinci

Watch It! (DVD Clip #1, 1 minute)

In this brief video segment, Lee Strobel introduces the discussion topic for this session. Use the following space to take a few notes.

Discuss It!

1 Compare and contrast the book, *The Da Vinci Code*, with the movie based on it. Which did you like better? Why?

2 Throughout *The Da Vinci Code*, a concept called the "sacred feminine" is referenced. Describe what you think the "sacred feminine" is all about. Do you have a positive, negative, or neutral viewpoint toward the idea? Explain.

Claim vs. Counterclaim

"Powerful men in the early Christian church 'conned' the world by propagating lies that devalued the female. . . . Constantine and his male successors successfully converted the world from matriarchal paganism to patriarchal Christianity by waging a campaign of propaganda that demonized the sacred feminine." (p. 124)

The Da Vinci Code

"Nowhere in serious scholarly work do we find anyone taking seriously the suggestion that Jesus' mission was all about sending forth Mary Magdalene to carry his message of the 'sacred feminine.' "

Amy Welborn in De-Coding Da Vinci

Breathtaking Nonsense?

"There is no convincing evidence for . . . Israelite men coming to the temple to experience the divine and achieve spiritual wholeness by having sex with priestesses. . . . Brown explains that the Holy of Holies 'housed not only God but also His powerful female equal, Shekinah.' A word not found in the Bible but in later rabbinic writings, *Shekinah* refers to the nearness of God to his people and not to a female consort. . . . It is also breathtaking nonsense to assert as a 'fact' that the sacred tetragrammaton, YHWH, was 'derived from Jehovah, an androgynous physical union between the masculine *Jah* and the pre-Hebraic name for Eve, *Havah*.' "

Gerald O'Collins, Jesuit Scripture scholar

Watch It! (DVD Clip #2, 7 minutes)

Use the following space to take notes as Lee Strobel interviews Kathy McReynolds on: the suppression of women in the church, the story behind original sin, and the "sacred feminine." Dr. McReynolds earned her doctorate in religion and social ethics at the University of Southern California and teaches at Biola University in La Mirada, California. She is coauthor of *Women as Christ's Disciples*, which examines Mary Magdalene and other women who were followers of Jesus.

Discuss It!

3 *The Da Vinci Code* charges that over the past two thousand years, Christianity has been virulently patriarchal, anti-woman, and determined to stamp out any hints of the "sacred feminine." To what extent do you agree or disagree with this allegation and why? Explain.

4 *The Da Vinci Code* says: "It was *man*, not God, who created the concept of 'original sin,' whereby Eve tasted of the apple and caused the downfall of the human race. Woman, once the sacred giver of life, was now the enemy" (p. 238). To what extent do you think Eve caused humanity's downfall? Does the Bible hold Eve or the whole human race responsible for original sin? Explain. In what ways does the church view women as the enemy?

Not the Enemy?

"Christianity does not declare that Eve caused humanity's downfall. The church teaches that the Fall came through Eve and Adam — particularly Adam because he deliberately chose to disobey God. Hence, the Bible teaches that 'since by a man came death, by a man also came the resurrection.... For as in Adam all die, so also in Christ all will be made alive' (1 Corinthians 15:21–22). Furthermore, according to Christianity women are not the enemy of mankind. Jesus and his followers consistently sought to elevate women to a place of equality with men."

Robert Abanes in *The Truth Behind the Da Vinci Code*

5 Read and compare the following two excerpts:

"The Catholic Inquisition published the ... *Malleus Maleficarum* — or *The Witches' Hammer* — (which) indoctrinated the world to 'the dangers of freethinking women' and instructed the clergy how to locate, torture, and destroy them.... During three hundred years of witch hunts, the Church burned at the stake an astounding five *million* women." (p. 125)

The Da Vinci Code

"This medieval book ... was used to persecute both women *and men*. In fact, historical documents show that most of the victims 'were not killed by Catholics or officials of the Church,' but were executed by the state. Scholarly estimates put the number of 'witch hunt' victims in Europe from 1400 to 1800 (a period of 100 years longer than the 300 years the *Code* mentions) at 30,000 to 80,000.... Moreover 20 to 25 percent of those were male."

Richard Abanes in *The Truth Behind the Da Vinci Code*

What's your perspective on this period in the history of the church? Concerning the difference of opinions stated above, who do you agree with and why? How can the truth really be determined?

6 To what extent were women treated like second-class citizens in the past?

Breaking the Mold

"I agree that historically the church can be faulted for not giving women their rightful place in Christian ministry.... Jesus did reject those cultural taboos that put women in a disrespected place as second-class citizens of the Kingdom. Women in Scripture are equal with men, though their roles are different.... Jesus broke the mold, elevating women to a place of respect and honor."

Erwin Lutzer in *The Da Vinci Deception*

7 To what extent are women treated unfairly in our world today? In what ways do you think women are treated unfairly within Christianity?

Saint or Demon?

"Brown suggests, repeatedly, that Mary Magdalene was marginalized and demonized by traditional Christianity.... It simply makes no sense. Christianity, both East and West, has honored Mary Magdalene as a saint. They've named churches after her, prayed at her purported tombs before what was believed to be her relics, and ascribed miracles to her. How in the world, in what universe, is that demonizing? Answer: It's not."

Amy Welborn in _De-Coding Da Vinci_

8 *The Da Vinci Code* makes an argument that Mary Magdalene was "shunned" and "demonized" by the church? Do you agree with this charge? Why or why not?

An Eternal Debt?

"It seemed Eve's bite from the apple of knowledge was a debt women were doomed to pay for eternity." (p. 41)

The Da Vinci Code

Bizarre Omission?

"Apparently, Brown has never heard of Mary, the Mother of Jesus. If you really want to understand how distant this novel's assertions are from the truth about Christianity, reflect for a moment on that glaring, bizarre omission. And wonder why. One can only conclude that paying any heed to the tremendous import of Mary in Christian thought and expression would completely undermine Brown's contention that orthodox Christianity lives in mortal fear of the 'sacred feminine,' so he naturally thought it best to pretend it never happened."

Amy Welborn in *De-Coding Da Vinci*

9 *The Da Vinci Code* doesn't make mention of the role of Mary, the mother of Jesus. How do you explain this omission? What kind of influence and impact did the Virgin Mary have on the church and Christianity?

10 *The Da Vinci Code* says, *"The Last Supper* practically shouts at the viewer that Jesus and Magdalene were a pair" (p. 244). Do you agree with this assessment of Da Vinci's painting?

Watch It! (DVD Clip #3, 7 minutes)

Use the following space to take notes as Lee Strobel continues to interview scholar Kathy McReynolds on: Jesus' relationship with Mary Magdalene; Jesus' attitude toward women and their role in the church; the current state of affairs; and changes, if any, that should be implemented.

Discuss It!

11 *The Da Vinci Code* claims that the marriage of Jesus and Mary Magdalene is "part of the historical record" and that the chalice in the Grail legend actually refers to Mary Maglalene, whose womb supposedly carried Jesus' royal bloodline. Do you agree with this assessment? Why or why not?

Expected to Marry?

"Jesus was a Jew and the social decorum during that time virtually forbid a Jewish man to be unmarried.... If Jesus were not married, at least one of the Bible's gospels would have mentioned it." (p. 245)

The Da Vinci Code

"Marriage was certainly the rule and expectation for Jews. By the first century, there were exceptions to the rule.... It has long been believed by Christians and scholars that Jesus was single, and there are good reasons for this belief. When he was in ministry, there was no mention of a wife.... Jesus' family members—his mother, brothers, and sisters—were mentioned more than once, but never a wife. Nor was there any indication that he was widowed.... What was the likelihood that Jesus was married? The answer here is short—none."

Darrell Bock in *Breaking the Da Vinci Code*

12 Do you think it would have been a problem if Jesus actually had been married to Mary Magdalene? Why or why not? What if they had a child together?

A Theological Problem?

"I don't think there is anything wrong with the concept of Jesus being married. Marriage, after all, was invented by God. The problem is this: One of the functions of marriage is to produce children and that leads to a theological problem. Can't you see Jesus talking to his oldest son, saying, 'Well, Samuel, you are only one-quarter God and three-quarters man, and your son, Jacob, in turn, is only going to be one-eighth God.' We'd have a terrible theological problem. So I think it's much better that Jesus didn't get married. And he did not."

Historian Paul Maier

13 A central claim of *The Da Vinci Code* is that Jesus — "the original feminist" — gave Mary Magdalene instructions to carry on his church after he was gone, but that Peter — who was "something of a sexist" — foiled his plan. To what extent do you think Jesus is the original feminist? What evidence would you need to be convinced that he intended for Mary Magdalene to lead the church? Explain. What do you think was Jesus' view of women and their role in society and the church?

The Future Marriage of Jesus

"Of course, someday Jesus will be married. Jesus is now engaged to us, the church—his bride. He would not have been married on earth, knowing that his coming marriage is in heaven. On that day, we, along with Mary Magdalene, will be invited to the marriage supper of the Lamb, where the marriage is consummated, not in a physical sexual union, but in the most blessed and intimate union of fellowship imaginable."

Erwin Lutzer in *The Da Vinci Deception*

14 Describe how the Christian church has viewed the role of women in the past and how that as changed over the years.

15 If you were grading the church as a whole on how it has lived up to Jesus' attitudes toward women, what grade would you give and why?

16 What place do you think women should have in the church today? Why?

17 If you had the power to make sweeping changes in the church worldwide, what changes, if any, would you propose about the treatment of women in the church and the role they are given in it? Explain.

Watch It! (DVD Clip #4, 2 minutes)

Lee's Perspective

Jesus was a revolutionary in his attitudes toward women in a day when they were considered to have less than equal value. Said Rebecca Jones in her new book *Does Christianity Squash Women?*: "Jesus never slanders or belittles women. He does not make generalizations about them. He does not shut them out of conversations or ignore them. He doesn't make them feel small or relegate them to an inferior status. Everything he says and does in relation to women shows the utmost care and respect." Has the church always lived up to those ideals? Unfortunately, no. But that's a reflection on the human beings who run the institution, not on Jesus himself. Our eyes ought to be on him and his teachings.

Forget the revisionist history of *The Da Vinci Code*—reputable historians merely scoff at the idea that Jesus was married to Mary Magdalene and wanted her to head his church, since the evidence is nonexistent. Instead, both women *and* men can find hope in the real model of Christianity that's reflected in Galatians 3:28: "There is neither Jew nor Greek, slave nor free, male nor female, for you are all one in Christ Jesus."

IS JESUS THE SON OF GOD?

The noblest pleasure is the joy of understanding.
Leonardo da Vinci

Watch It! (DVD Clip #1, 1 minute)

In this brief video segment, Lee Strobel introduces the discussion topic for this session. Use the following space to take a few notes.

Discuss It!

1 Using the continuum below, who do you think Jesus was? Give reasons for your response.

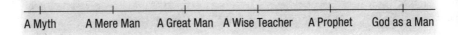

A Myth   A Mere Man   A Great Man   A Wise Teacher   A Prophet   God as a Man

2 *The Da Vinci Code* claims that Jesus' followers considered him to be "a great and powerful man," but a *man* nonetheless, and that it wasn't until the fourth century that the Emperor Constantine turned Jesus into a deity for his own nefarious purposes. If this is true, what are the implications for Christianity?

The Human Side of Jesus

The Da Vinci Code alleges that Emperor Constantine omitted gospels that portrayed the human side of Jesus. However, listed below are descriptions found in the four Gospels in the Bible. Read them to see how the New Testament affirms Jesus' human traits.

- He began life as a baby, born from a woman (Luke 2:6–7).
- He went through the development stages of childhood (Luke 2:52).
- He worked as a carpenter (Mark 6:3).
- He became hungry and thirsty (Matthew 4:2; John 19:28).
- He became tired and fatigued (Mark 4:38).
- He experienced sadness and sorrow (John 11:35).
- He became amazed (Matthew 8:10).
- He had limited knowledge (Mathew 24:36).
- He became angry (Mark 11:15–16; John 2:13–17).
- He became fearful of impending suffering (Matthew 26:38).
- He became disappointed (Matthew 26:40–45).
- He bled and died (John 19:33–34).

Watch It! (DVD Clip #2, 7 minutes)

Use the following space to take notes as Lee Strobel interviews New Testament scholar Mark Strauss on: *The Da Vinci Code's* claim that Jesus' identity was stolen, the *Code's* charge that Constantine destroyed gospels that portrayed Jesus as human, and Jesus' own claims about who he really was. Dr. Strauss, who earned his doctorate at the University of Aberdeen in Scotland, has been a professor for more than a dozen years at Bethel Seminary in San Diego. He has written numerous books and articles, including his most recent: *Four Portraits, One Jesus: An Introduction to Jesus and the Gospels.*

Discuss It!

3 According to *The Da Vinci Code*, Christianity as we know it today is essentially the work, not of Jesus and his disciples, but of Emperor Constantine, who reigned over the Roman Empire in the fourth century. To what extent is this true or false? Explain.

The Official Religion

"Church historians agree that next to the events in the New Testament, the most important event in the history of Christianity is the conversion of Emperor Constantine to Christianity in AD 312.... But did he invent the divinity of Jesus? Before the council (of Nicaea), was Christ believed to be just a remarkable man? There is not a single shred of historical evidence for such a notion."

Erwin Lutzer in *The Da Vinci Deception*

4 Jesus often referred to himself as the "Son of Man." According to Mark Strauss, what does this phrase mean? Does Strauss's analysis make sense to you? Why or why not?

5 According to the following biblical references, to what extent do you think Jesus claimed to be God? Explain.

- Jesus believed he would judge the world at the end of time (Matthew 7:21–23; John 5:22).
- Jesus believed he should be honored as much as God (John 5:23).
- Jesus believed he could impart eternal life to people (John 5:21, 39–40).
- Jesus believed that to see him was to see God (John 14:9).
- Jesus believed that to know him was to know God (John 8:19).
- Jesus believed that to hate him was to hate God (John 15:23).
- Jesus believed he could forgive sin (Mark 2:5, 10).
- Jesus accepted worship and being called "God" (John 20:28–29).
- Jesus claimed titles exclusive to God (John 8:56–58).
- Jesus claimed he and the Father were one (John 10:22–33).
- Jesus believed he had been with God in heaven and shared divine glory (John 17:5).
- Jesus believed he could hear and answer prayers (John 14:14).
- After the resurrection, Jesus believed he was omnipresent (Matthew 28:20; John 14:23).

6 If Jesus didn't want us to conclude he was God, how could he have made that clear? Do you know of any example when he attempted to deny his divinity?

Watch It! (DVD Clip #3, 7 minutes)

Use the following space to take notes as Lee Strobel continues his interview with New Testament expert Mark Strauss on: who Jesus' earliest followers thought he was, the evidence supporting the deity of Jesus, and how to understand the idea that Jesus was fully human *and* fully God.

Discuss It!

7 According to Mark Strauss, who did Jesus' earliest followers think he was? Do you agree with Strauss's perspective? Why or why not?

Deciding Divinity?

"The Council of Nicaea had nothing to do with *deciding* Jesus' divinity. By the end of his earthly ministry, Christ's divinity was already being acknowledged. The Jews who chose to reject Jesus understood very well his claims, which they described as making himself out to be God."

Richard Abanes in *The Truth Behind the Da Vinci Code*

Considered Divine Before AD 325?

Long before the Council of Nicaea, people considered Jesus divine:

- Ignatius: "God Himself was manifested in human form" (AD 105).
- Clement: "It is fitting that you should think of Jesus Christ as of God" (AD 150).
- Justin Martyr: "Being the first-begotten Word of God, is even God"; "Both God and Lord of hosts"; "The Father of the universe has a Son. And He ... is even God" (AD 160).
- Irenaeus: "Our Lord, and God, and Savior, and King"; "He is God, for the name Emmanuel indicates this" (AD 180).
- Tertullian: "Christ our God" (AD 200).
- Origen: "No one should be offended that the Savior is also God" (AD 225).
- Novatian: "He is not only man, but God also" (AD 235).
- Cyprian: "Jesus Christ, our Lord and God" (AD 250).
- Methodius: "He truly was and is ... with God, and being God" (AD 290).
- Lactantius: "We believe Him to be God" (AD 304).
- Arnobius: "Christ performed all these miracles ... the duty of Divinity" (AD 305).

James Garlow and Peter Jones in *Cracking Da Vinci's Code*

8 Anyone can claim to be God, but Jesus actually convinced his followers that he was telling the truth about his divine identity by:

- Performing miracles (both the Jewish Talmud and the Islamic Koran concede he worked the supernatural).
- Living a sinless life (two of his closest companions, John and Peter, observed his moral perfection; see 1 John 3:5 and 1 Peter 2:22).
- Fulfilling ancient messianic prophecies against all mathematical odds.
- Resurrecting from the dead.

Do you believe these arguments provide convincing evidence that Jesus was God incarnate? Why or why not?

9 Jesus' identity is a difficult concept to grasp. How do you explain the idea that Jesus was fully human *and* fully God?

"Jesus made it clear by word and deed that to know him was to know God, to see him was to see God, to believe in him was to believe in God, to receive him was to receive God, to reject him was to reject God, and to honor him was to honor God."

British pastor John Stott

10 Some people find the idea that God came and lived among us very exciting and hopeful. Yet, history shows a widespread hostility to this belief. Why does his deity spark such opposition?

Faith in Jesus?

"Modern Christianity may certainly be diverse, but at the core of all Christian faith is the belief that Jesus, fully divine and fully human, is the One through whom God reconciled the world—and each one of us—to Himself, and that salvation is found through faith in Jesus, who is not dead but lives."

Amy Welborn in *De-Coding Da Vinci*

11 What aspect of Jesus' divinity is difficult or troublesome for you to accept? Why?

12 If it were true that Jesus really was God in the flesh, what are some implications for *your* life today?

A Great Human Teacher?

"Either this man was, and is, the Son of God: or else a madman or something worse. You can shut him up for a fool, you can spit at him and kill him as a demon; or you can fall at his feet and call him Lord and God. But let us not come with any patronizing nonsense about him being a great human teacher. He has not left that open to us. He did not intend to."

C. S. Lewis

13 Read John 20:28–31. Thomas had doubts about Jesus until he saw him resurrected in person and said, "My Lord and my God!" What do you think it would take (or what did it take) for you to draw the same conclusion about Jesus?

Watch It! (DVD Clip #4, 2 minutes)

Lee's Perspective

Everything comes down to this one central issue: was Jesus a mere human being who was later deified by Emperor Constantine? If so, then Christianity is a sham. Or is he the unique Son of God—and if so, doesn't he then deserve our worship and allegiance?

In my opinion, the evidence for his deity is powerful and persuasive. First, he clearly claimed to be divine—even in the earliest gospel—and his opponents accused him of blasphemy for daring to equate himself with God. Second, he backed up those claims by rising from the dead. To me, the evidence for the resurrection is compelling and convincing. Everyone in the ancient world agreed his tomb was empty. He appeared alive to more than 515 eyewitnesses, including skeptics whose lives were revolutionized as a result. The report of his resurrection comes so early that it simply cannot be the product of legend. Finally, there's the willingness of the disciples to die for their conviction that Jesus came back to life. They didn't just *believe* the resurrection was true; they were in a unique position to *know* firsthand that it actually occurred. Nobody knowingly and willingly dies for a lie.

Compared to this avalanche of evidence, Dan Brown offers nothing with any credibility to support his allegations. Friends, the verdict of history is clear: Jesus is who he claimed to be. And that leads to the most important question of all: how should you and I respond to him?

APPENDIXES

Appendix 1

RECOMMENDED RESOURCES

Abanes, Richard. *The Truth Behind the Da Vinci Code*. Eugene, Ore.: Harvest House, 2004.
Abanes is an award-winning author on the cults and world religions.

Bock, Darrell L. *Breaking the Da Vinci Code*. Nashville: Thomas Nelson, 2004.
Bock is research professor of New Testament studies at Dallas Theological Seminary.

Garlow, James L. and Peter Jones. *Cracking Da Vinci's Code*. Colorado Springs: Victor, 2004.
Garlow has a doctorate in historical theology from Drew University; Jones has a doctorate from Princeton Theological Seminary.

Hanegraaff, Hank and Paul L. Maier. *The Da Vinci Code: Fact or Fiction*. Wheaton, Ill.: Tyndale, 2004.
Hanegraaff hosts the national Bible Answer Man *radio show; Maier is a professor of ancient history at Western Michigan University.*

Lutzer, Erwin W. *The Da Vinci Deception*. Wheaton, Ill.: Tyndale, 2004.
Lutzer is senior pastor of the historic Moody Church in Chicago.

Olson, Carl E. and Sandra Miesel. *The Da Vinci Hoax*. San Francisco: Ignatius Press, 2004.
Olson is a Catholic author and contributor to First Things. *Miesel is a journalist with a master's degree in medieval history from the University of Illinois.*

Strobel, Lee. *The Case for Christ*. Grand Rapids, Mich.: Zondervan, 1998.
Strobel is an atheist-turned-Christian, former legal editor of the Chicago Tribune, *and* New York Times *bestselling author.*

Welborn, Amy. *De-Coding Da Vinci*. Huntington, Ind.: Our Sunday Visitor, 2004.
Welborn holds a master's degree in church history from Vanderbilt University.

Witherington, Ben III. *The Gospel Code*. Downers Grove, Ill.: InterVarsity Press, 2004.
Witherington is professor of New Testament at Asbury Theological Seminary in Wilmore, Kentucky.

www.discussingthedavincicode.com

Appendix 2

FAQS ABOUT
THE DA VINCI CODE

Mark L. Strauss, PhD
Bethel Seminary San Diego

(©2006 by Mark L. Strauss. All rights reserved.)

The Da Vinci Code *claims:*

- Almost everything the church teaches about Jesus is false.
- Jesus was only human. No one claimed he was divine until a church council in the fourth century declared him to be a god.
- Jesus was married to Mary Magdalene.
- Mary was pregnant when Jesus was crucified.
- Their offspring are alive today, a secret kept by the Priory of Sion.
- Mary herself is the "Holy Grail."
- Mary appears in Leonardo Da Vinci's painting *The Last Supper.*
- Earliest Christianity worshiped the divine feminine. The later church suppressed this.
- The Gospels (Matthew, Mark, Luke, and John) are just four among eighty or so other gospels. These other gospels, which described Jesus' relationship to Mary, were suppressed by the church. History, says author Dan Brown, is written by the winners.

Was Jesus' deity created by the church in the fourth century?

- The Council of Nicea in AD 325 debated important issues, and confirmed Jesus' deity. But it did not create it! Christians had been worshiping Jesus and proclaiming his deity for centuries.
- The New Testament already explicitly claims Jesus' deity. (See, for example, John 1:1; Colossians 1:15; Hebrews 1:3.)

Who was Mary Magdalene?

There are many legends, only a few certainties:
- One of the women who supported Jesus (Luke 8:1–3).
- A recipient of Jesus' exorcism (Luke 8:2).
- The first witness to the resurrection (John 20:10–18).
- Not a prostitute and unlikely the woman caught in adultery (John 8:1–11).

Was Jesus married to Mary Magdalene?

- Though Jewish men of Jesus' day were usually married, there were many exceptions. For example:
  - The Essenes of the Dead Sea community at Qumran remained single.
  - The apostle Paul was single (1 Corinthians 7:7).
  - In both Judaism and Christianity, singleness and celibacy were esteemed as a means to complete devotion to the Lord (1 Corinthians 7:32–33).
  - While most rabbis were married, Jesus more closely fulfilled the role of a prophet. Prophets often remained single to be wholly devoted to the Lord.
  - John the Baptist, the prophet and forerunner of the Messiah, was unmarried.
- All of the evidence indicates Jesus was single.
  - Jesus said the Son of Man had no place to lay his head (Matthew 8:20; Luke 9:58).
  - From the cross, Jesus commends his mother to John's care, but does not mention a wife.
  - There is no hint of any sexual or marital relationship between Jesus and the women who supported him.
- There is not a shred of early or reliable historical evidence that Jesus was married.

Does Mary Magdalene appear in Da Vinci's Last Supper?

- Art historians recognize this as John the apostle, not Mary Magdalene.
- John the apostle is not seen elsewhere in the painting.
- John is often depicted in art as a young, feminine-looking man.
- In early sketches, Da Vinci himself identified this as John, not Mary.

Were the four Gospels of the Bible arbitrarily chosen from among more than eighty contenders?

- The New Testament Gospels are by far the oldest and most reliable records we have of the historical Jesus.
- The so-called "apocryphal gospels" were written decades (most, centuries) after the New Testament Gospels.
- The vast majority of "apocryphal gospels" are very late, fanciful, and dependent on the four Gospels.
- The few outside sources we have confirm the picture of Jesus found in the Gospels (see Josephus, *Antiquities* 18.3.3 §§63–64).

Is the Bible a merely human book?

- It is true that the Bible did not drop from heaven. No scholar claims it did.
- The Bible claims to be inspired by God, with human authors communicating God's message.
- Translations today come from very early Greek and Hebrew manuscripts (not "countless" versions).
- We have extraordinarily reliable manuscripts, very close to the originals.
- The divine origin of the Bible is confirmed by fulfilled prophecy and its transforming power.

Did the pagan Roman emperor Constantine choose which books to put in the Bible?

- Constantine converted to Christianity, so he was not a "pagan" emperor.
- Constantine had nothing to do with which books were included in the Bible.
- The New Testament books were considered inspired Scripture long before Constantine was born.

Are the Dead Sea Scrolls "lost gospels"?

- The Dead Sea Scrolls are Jewish, not Christian writings, written a hundred-plus years before Jesus was born. They have nothing to do with him.
- Jesus is (of course) never mentioned in these scrolls.

Are the Gnostic gospels the earliest Christian records?

- Almost all scholars date the Gnostic gospels to the second century or later, and consider them to be dependent on the four New Testament Gospels. They are certainly not the earliest Christian records.
- The suggestion that Jesus was originally a Gnostic does not fit his historical context. Jesus was a first-century Palestinian Jew (everyone agrees on this), and his earliest followers were Palestinian Jews. The New Testament Gospels place Jesus accurately in this first-century Jewish context.
- The Gnostic literature does not fit this historical background, suggesting that it was a later development that arose under the influence of Greek philosophical thought.

Does the Gnostic Gospel of Philip *reveal Jesus' marital relationship with Mary Magdalene?*

- The *Gospel of Philip* is dated to the third century AD and has no legitimate claim to authenticity.
- The identification of Mary as Jesus' companion is part of a Gnostic worldview that spirit beings exist in male and female forms.

Was the early church misogynist and did it suppress women?

- Jesus highly valued women, raising them to the position of disciples or close followers (consider Mary and Martha in Luke 10:38–42). A group of women supported his ministry.
- Women receive a higher place in the church than in the pagan world or in Judaism (consider Lydia, Priscilla, Phoebe, and Junia).
- Pagan goddess worship generally "used" women. It did not exalt them.
- The Gnostic documents themselves are misogynist. For example, in the *Gospel of Thomas*, Jesus says of Mary, "I myself shall lead her in order to make her

male. . . . For every woman who will make herself male will enter the Kingdom of Heaven."

Has Jesus' royal bloodline (through Mary Magdalene) been documented by many reputable historians?

- This "historical fact" has no validity and is not supported by any real historians.
- It has been promoted in the book, *Holy Blood, Holy Grail*, by Michael Baigent, Richard Leigh, and Henry Lincoln, none of whom are historians or scholars.

Do Christian symbols have pagan origins?

- It is certainly true that Christians took over pagan symbols and "baptized" them with Christian meaning.
- The real question is: *Is the new meaning Christian or pagan?*

Was Sunday worship started by Constantine as part of the worship of the sun?

- This is false. The New Testament shows Christians worshiping on the first day of the week (Sunday) during the first century (Acts 20:7; 1 Corinthians 16:2; Revelation 1:10).
- Christians worshiped on Sunday because it was the day of the resurrection.

Appendix 3

EVIDENCE FOR THE TRUE IDENTITY OF JESUS

Lee Strobel

The Da Vinci Code paints Jesus as being a mere human being who was turned into a god almost three hundred years after his death by Emperor Constantine for the ruler's own selfish purposes. However, that's not what I discovered during my own spiritual investigation into Jesus' identity. As an atheist, I spent two years checking out Jesus and coming to the conclusion that he is the unique Son of God. Here is a summary of the historical evidence for Jesus Christ from thirteen leading experts who were interviewed for my book *The Case for Christ*:

Can the biographies of Jesus be trusted?

I once thought that the Gospels were merely religious propaganda, hopelessly tainted by overactive imaginations and evangelistic zeal. But Craig Blomberg of Denver Seminary, one of the country's foremost authorities on the biographies of Jesus, built a convincing case that they reflect eyewitness testimony and bear the unmistakable earmarks of accuracy. So early are these accounts of Jesus' life that they cannot be explained away as legendary inventions. "Within the first two years after his death," Blomberg said, "significant numbers of Jesus' followers seem to have formulated a doctrine of the atonement, were convinced that he had been raised from the dead in bodily form, associated Jesus with God, and believed they found support for all these convictions in the Old Testament." A study indicates that there was nowhere near enough time for legend to have developed and wiped out a solid core of historical truth.

Do Jesus' biographies stand up to scrutiny?

Blomberg argued persuasively that the Gospel writers intended to preserve reliable history; were able to do so; were honest and willing to include difficult-to-explain material; and didn't allow bias to unduly color their reporting. The harmony among the Gospels on essential facts, coupled with divergence on some incidental details, lends historical credibility to the accounts. What's more, the early church could not have taken root and flourished right there in Jerusalem if it had been teaching facts about Jesus that his own contemporaries could have exposed as exaggerated or false. In short, the Gospels were able to pass all eight evidential tests, demonstrating their basic trustworthiness as historical records.

Were Jesus' biographies reliably preserved for us?

World-class scholar Bruce Metzger, professor emeritus at Princeton Theological Seminary, said that compared to other ancient documents, there is an unprecedented number of New Testament manuscripts and that they can be dated extremely close to the original writings. The modern New Testament is 99.5 percent free of textual discrepancies, with no major Christian doctrine in doubt. The criteria used by the early church to determine which books should be considered authoritative have ensured that we possess the best records about Jesus.

Is there credible evidence for Jesus outside his biographies?

"We have better historical documentation for Jesus than for the founder of any other ancient religion," said Edwin Yamauchi of Miami University, a leading expert on ancient history. Sources from outside the Bible corroborate that many people believed Jesus performed healings and was the Messiah; that he was crucified; and that despite this shameful death, his followers, who believed he was still alive, worshiped him as God. One expert documented thirty-nine ancient sources that corroborate more than one hundred facts concerning Jesus' life, teachings, crucifixion, and resurrection. Seven secular sources and several early Christian creeds concern the deity of Jesus, a doctrine "definitely present in the earliest church," according to Dr. Gary Habermas, the scholar who wrote *The Historical Jesus.*

Does archaeology confirm or contradict Jesus' biographies?

John McRay, a professor of archaeology for more than fifteen years and author of *Archaeology and the New Testament,* said there's no question that archaeological findings have enhanced the New Testament's credibility. No discovery has ever disproved a biblical reference. Further, archaeology has established that Luke, who wrote about one-quarter of the New Testament, was an especially careful historian. Concluded one expert: "If Luke was so painstakingly accurate in his historical reporting [of minor details], on what logical basis may we assume he was credulous or inaccurate in his reporting of matters that were far more important, not only to him but to others as well?" Like, for instance, the resurrection of Jesus—the event that authenticated his claim to being the unique Son of God.

Is the Jesus of history the same as the Jesus of faith?

Gregory Boyd, a Yale- and Princeton-educated scholar who wrote the award-winning *Cynic Sage or Son of God?,* offered a devastating critique of the Jesus Seminar, a group that questions whether Jesus said or did most of what's attributed to him. He identified the Seminar as "an extremely small number of radical-fringe scholars who are on the far, far left wing of New Testament thinking." The Seminar ruled out the possibility of miracles at the outset, employed questionable criteria, and some participants have touted myth-riddled documents of extremely dubious quality. Further, the idea that stories about Jesus emerged from mythology fails to withstand scrutiny. In sum, the Jesus of faith is the same as the Jesus of history.

Was Jesus really convinced he was the Son of God?

By going back to the very earliest traditions, which were unquestionably safe from legendary development, Ben Witherington III, author of *The Christology of Jesus,* was able to show that Jesus had a supreme and transcendent self-understanding. Based on the evidence, Witherington said: "Did Jesus believe he was the Son of God, the anointed one of God? The answer is yes. Did he see himself as the Son of Man? The answer is yes. Did he see himself as the final Messiah? Yes, that's the way he viewed himself. Did he believe that anybody less than God could save the world? No, I don't believe he did." Scholars said that Jesus' repeated reference to himself as the Son of Man was not a claim of humanity, but a reference to Daniel 7:13–14, in which the Son of Man is seen as having universal authority and everlasting dominion and who receives the worship of all nations. Said one scholar: "Thus, the claim to be the Son of Man would be in effect a claim to divinity."

Was Jesus crazy when he claimed to be the Son of God?

Gary Collins, a professor of psychology for twenty years and author of forty-five books on psychology-related topics, said Jesus exhibited no inappropriate emotions; was in contact with reality; was brilliant and had amazing insights into human nature; and enjoyed deep and abiding relationships. "I just don't see signs that Jesus was suffering from any known mental illness," he concluded. In addition, Jesus backed up his claim to being God through miraculous feats of healing; astounding demonstrations of power over nature; unrivaled teaching; divine understanding of people; and with his own resurrection, which was the ultimate evidence of his deity.

Did Jesus fulfill the attributes of God?

While the incarnation — God becoming man, the infinite becoming finite — stretches our imaginations, prominent theologian D. A. Carson pointed out that there's lots of evidence that Jesus exhibited the characteristics of deity. Based on Philippians 2, many theologians believe Jesus voluntarily emptied himself of the independent use of his divine attributes as he pursued his mission of human redemption. Even so, the New Testament specifically confirms that Jesus ultimately possessed every qualification of deity, including omniscience, omnipresence, omnipotence, eternality, and immutability.

Did Jesus — and Jesus alone — match the identity of the Messiah?

Hundreds of years before Jesus was born, prophets foretold the coming of the Messiah, or the Anointed One, who would redeem God's people. In effect, dozens of these Old Testament prophecies created a fingerprint that only the true Messiah could fit. This gave Israel a way to rule out imposters and validate the credentials of the authentic Messiah. Against astronomical odds — by one estimate, one chance in a trillion, trillion, trillion, trillion, trillion, trillion, trillion, trillion, trillion, trillion, trillion, trillion — Jesus, and only Jesus throughout history, matched this prophetic fingerprint. This confirms

90

Jesus' identity to an incredible degree of certainty. The expert I interviewed on this topic, Louis Lapides, is an example of someone raised in a conservative Jewish home who came to believe Jesus is the Messiah after a systematic study of the prophecies. Today, he's pastor of a church in California and former president of a national network of fifteen messianic congregations.

Was Jesus' death a sham, and his resurrection a hoax?

By analyzing the medical and historical data, Dr. Alexander Metherell, a physician who also holds a doctorate in engineering, concluded Jesus could not have survived the gruesome rigors of crucifixion, much less the gaping wound that pierced his lung and heart. In fact, even before the crucifixion he was in serious to critical condition and suffering from hypovolemic shock as the result of a horrific flogging. The idea that he swooned on the cross and pretended to be dead lacks any evidential basis. Roman executioners were grimly efficient, knowing that they themselves would face death if any of their victims were to come down from the cross alive. Even if Jesus had somehow lived through the torture, his ghastly condition could never have inspired a worldwide movement based on the premise that he had gloriously triumphed over the grave.

Was Jesus' body really absent from his tomb?

William Lane Craig, who has earned two doctorates and written several books on the resurrection, presented striking evidence that the enduring symbol of Easter — the vacant tomb of Jesus — was a historical reality. The empty grave is reported or implied in extremely early sources — Mark's gospel and a creed in 1 Corinthians 15 — which date so close to the event that they could not possibly have been products of legend. The fact that the Gospels report that women discovered the empty tomb bolsters the story's authenticity, because women's testimony lacked credibility in the first century and thus there would have been no motive to report they found the empty tomb if it weren't true. The site of Jesus' tomb was known to Christians, Jews, and Romans, so it could have been checked by skeptics. In fact, nobody — not even the Roman authorities or Jewish leaders — ever claimed that the tomb still contained Jesus' body. Instead, they were forced to invent the absurd story that the disciples, despite having no motive or opportunity, had stolen the body — a theory that not even the most skeptical critic believes today.

Was Jesus seen alive after his death on the cross?

The evidence for the post-resurrection appearances of Jesus didn't develop gradually over the years as mythology distorted memories of his life. Rather, said renowned resurrection expert Gary Habermas, his resurrection was "the central proclamation of the early church from the very beginning." The ancient creed from 1 Corinthians 15 mentions specific individuals who encountered the risen Christ, and Paul, in effect, challenged first-century doubters to talk with these individuals personally to determine the truth of the matter for themselves. The book of Acts is littered with extremely early affirmations of Jesus' resurrection, while the Gospels describe numerous encounters in detail. Concluded British theologian Michael Green: "The appearances of Jesus are as well authenticated as anything in antiquity.... There can be no rational doubt that they occurred."

Are there any supporting facts that point toward the resurrection?

Professor J. P. Moreland presented circumstantial evidence that provided strong documentation for the resurrection. First, the disciples were in a unique position to know whether the resurrection happened, and they went to their deaths proclaiming it was true. Nobody knowingly and willingly dies for a lie. Second, apart from the resurrection, there's no good reason why such skeptics as Paul and James would have been converted and would have died for their faith. Third, within weeks of the crucifixion, thousands of Jews became convinced Jesus was the Son of God and began following him, abandoning key social practices that had critical sociological and religious importance for centuries. They believed they risked damnation if they were wrong. Fourth, the early sacraments of Communion and baptism affirmed Jesus' resurrection and deity. And fifth, the miraculous emergence of the church in the face of brutal Roman persecution "rips a great hole in history, a hole the size and shape of resurrection," as C. F. D. Moule put it.

Taken together, I concluded that this expert testimony constitutes compelling evidence that Jesus Christ was who he claimed to be—the one and only Son of God. For details that support this summary, as well as other evidence, please refer to *The Case for Christ.*

Appendix 4

FOR LEADERS ONLY

If you are leading a small group through *Discussing the Da Vinci Code*, please use the following sample session overview as your guide. Each of the sessions is planned for approximately sixty minutes. NOTE: If you haven't already read the "Getting Started" section on pages 9–14, you'll find helpful leader information there as well. And don't forget to visit the Web site: *www.discussingthedavincicode.com*.

Before You Lead

If possible, read Dan Brown's *The Da Vinci Code* (Doubleday) if you haven't already, or reread it if your prior reading wasn't recent. And, of course, it also would be ideal to see the movie—perhaps with your group! It's possible your group will include members who have both read the book and seen the movie, have done one or the other, or perhaps have done neither to this point (but are just curious because of all the buzz).

Materials Needed

- Television monitor
- DVD player
- Watch or clock with which to monitor time
- The guide *Discussing the Da Vinci Code* (one per group member)
- Bible (modern translation such as the New International Version)
- Pen or pencil for everyone

Session Overview

Welcome (1 minute)

Welcome the group members and open in prayer if you would like.

Watch It! (1 minute)

Play the session's first DVD clip, always an introduction of the topic by Lee Strobel.

Discuss It! (5 minutes)

After the first DVD segment has played, lead the group in a discussion of the opening questions in the session.

Watch It! (7 minutes)

Play the session's second DVD clip, the first installment of an interview between Lee Strobel and a noted expert on the topic.

Discuss It! (18 minutes)

Lead a group discussion based on the next set of questions in the guide.

Watch It! (7 minutes)

Play the session's third DVD clip, the final installment of the interview between Lee Strobel and his guest.

Discuss It! (18 minutes)

Again, as a group, interact with the next set of questions in the guide.

Watch It! (2 minutes)

Each session ends with a DVD clip entitled "Lee's Perspective," where Lee Strobel draws his own conclusions regarding the topic and urges group members to do the same. A written version of "Lee's Perspective" also appears in the guide.

Wrap-up (1 minute)

Remind group members of the time and specifics of the next meeting and bring the session to a close.

ABOUT THE AUTHORS

Lee Strobel

Atheist-turned-Christian Lee Strobel is a *New York Times* bestselling author of nearly twenty books and has been featured on Fox News, CNN, ABC's *20/20*, and other national television and radio programs. Described by the *Washington Post* as "one of the evangelical community's most popular apologists," Lee won Gold Medallions for *The Case for Christ*, *The Case for Faith*, and *The Case for a Creator*. He earned a Master of Studies in Law degree from Yale Law School and was a journalist for fourteen years at the *Chicago Tribune* and other newspapers, winning Illinois' top honors for investigative reporting (which he shared with a team he led) and public service journalism from United Press International. He and his wife live in Southern California.

Garry Poole

Garry Poole, director of spiritual discovery at Willow Creek Community Church in South Barrington, Illinois, is a leading innovator of small groups designed to help spiritual seekers investigate Christianity. His award-winning book *Seeker Small Groups* provides a detailed blueprint for implementing this highly successful ministry. Garry authored (with Lee Strobel) *Experiencing the Passion of Jesus* to accompany Mel Gibson's movie *The Passion of the Christ*. In 2005, it became the first discussion guide ever to receive the prestigious Charles "Kip" Jordon Christian Book of the Year award. Garry also wrote *The Complete Book of Questions* and is coauthor of the bestselling Tough Questions series of discussion guides. He consults on seeker groups at churches around the world. Garry lives in suburban Chicago.

Faith Under Fire Series

Lee Strobel and Garry Poole

Using video clips from the popular PAX-TV program Faith Under Fire, this cutting-edge DVD curriculum features spirited discussions between well-respected Christians, people of other faiths, or people with no faith at all on important spiritual and social issues. Host Lee Strobel, bestselling author of *The Case for Christ*, *The Case for Faith*, and *The Case for a Creator*, provides additional comments to guide small group discussion.

> *Guests include:* Rick Warren, Randy Alcorn, William Lane Craig, J. P. Moreland, Hugh Hewitt, Henry Cloud, Ergun Caner, Stephen Meyer, Albert Mohler, and more.

Each volume contains a four-session DVD and leader's guide, and is intended to be used in conjunction with a corresponding participant's guide (sold separately).

Faith Under Fire™ 1:
Faith & Jesus
Four sessions on Jesus,
the resurrection, universalism,
and the supernatural
DVD: 0-310-26828-1
Participant's Guide: 0-310-26829-X

Faith Under Fire™ 2:
Faith & Facts
Four sessions on the Bible,
heaven, hell, and science
DVD: 0-310-26850-8
Participant's Guide: 0-310-26851-6

Faith Under Fire™ 3:
Tough Faith Questions
Four sessions on forgiveness,
pain and suffering, the Trinity,
and Islam
DVD: 0-310-26855-9
Participant's Guide: 0-310-26856-7

Faith Under Fire™ 4:
A New Kind of Faith
Four sessions on the relevance
of Christianity
DVD: 0-310-26859-1
Participant's Guide: 0-310-26860-5